Richard Schlesinger
Kennesaw State University

VISUAL BASIC .NET

Programming Language

the

JONES AND BARTLETT PUBLISHERS

Sudbury, Massachusetts

BOSTON   TORC

World Headquarters
Jones and Bartlett Publishers
40 Tall Pine Drive
Sudbury, MA 01776
978-443-5000
info@jbpub.com
www.jbpub.com

Jones and Bartlett Publishers Canada
6339 Ormindale Way
Mississauga, Ontario L5V 1J2
CANADA

Jones and Bartlett Publishers International
Barb House, Barb Mews
London W6 7PA
UK

Jones and Bartlett's books and products are available through most bookstores and online book-sellers. To contact Jones and Bartlett Publishers directly, call 800-832-0034, fax 978-443-8000, or visit our website, www.jbpub.com.

Substantial discounts on bulk quantities of Jones and Bartlett's publications are available to corporations, professional associations, and other qualified organizations. For details and specific discount information, contact the special sales department at Jones and Bartlett via the above contact information or send an email to specialsales@jbpub.com.

Production Credits
Acquisitions Editor: Tim Anderson
Production Director: Amy Rose
Editorial Assistant: Laura Pagluica
Production Assistant: Mike Boblitt
Manufacturing Buyer: Therese Connell
Marketing Manager: Andrea DeFronzo
Composition: Northeast Compositors, Inc.
Cover Design: Kristin E. Ohlin
Cover Image: © Julien Tromeur/ShutterStock, Inc.
Printing and Binding: Malloy, Inc.
Cover Printing: Malloy, Inc.

6048

ISBN-13: 978-0-7637-5060-2
ISBN-10: 0-7637-5060-3

Printed in the United States of America
11 10 09 08 07   10 9 8 7 6 5 4 3 2 1

Visual Basic .Net: The Programming Language

After completing this chapter, you should be able to do the following:

- Describe how to use the Visual Basic IDE
- Describe the most commonly used screen objects
- Describe the various built-in data types
- Implement statements that declare and change the values of variables
- Implement statements that manipulate the properties of screen objects
- Implement conditional statements in Visual Basic
- Implement looping statements in Visual Basic
- Describe the use of subroutines and functions
- Explain how Visual Basic passes parameters
- Explain what *Events* are and how they work
- Implement statements that work with *Arrays* and *ArrayLists*
- Implement statements that use built-in classes
- Write your own classes
- Explain *encapsulation*, *inheritance*, and *polymorphism*
- Use graphics drawing methods to create simple screen drawings

Visual Basic .Net is an object-oriented language with imperative features. Additionally, it has an *interactive development environment* (IDE) that simplifies the development of forms (windows) to be displayed on a screen. We begin by examining this development environment and then exploring the language features for working with the screen objects created with the IDE.

1.1 Using Visual Basic

Visual Basic provides an *interactive development environment* (IDE) that helps simplify writing the program, compiling, and testing, as illustrated in Figure 1.

The IDE handles the numerous details of programming so you don't have to deal with them. Let's take a look at the IDE. When you start Visual Basic, the *Startup Screen* (Figure 2) appears. In the upper box on the left, there will be a list of the *Projects* (or programs) that you are working on. To create a new project, click on the *Create Project* button. The dialog box in Figure 3 will appear. Be sure that the template for *Windows Application* is selected. The dialog box will have a default name for the project. Replace this with the name you wish to use and click OK.

When you do this, the IDE will create the framework for a simple application and the *Design Screen* in Figure 4 will appear. This screen has several important elements:

- When your application runs, it will appear on the screen in a window that Visual Basic calls a *Form*. A template for how that form will look is in the center left of the *Main Window*. At this time, the form (and resulting window) is empty.
- The upper-right box of the screen is the *Solution Explorer* window, which shows the files that are part of this program. The file that is currently being displayed in the main window will be highlighted under *Solution Explorer*.

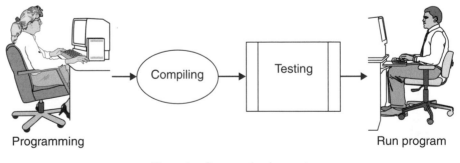

Programming   Run program

Figure 1   *Program development.*

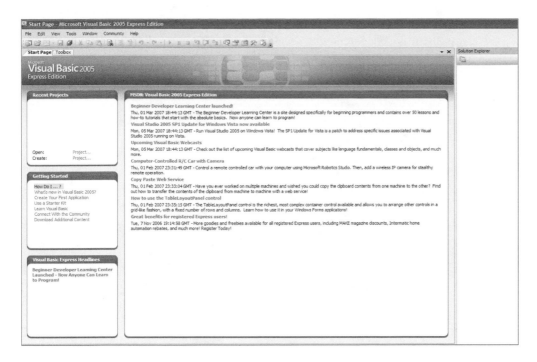

Figure 2   *Visual Basic startup screen.*

Figure 3   *New Project dialog.*

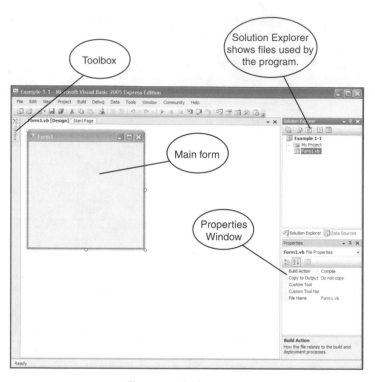

Figure 4 *Design screen.*

- The bottom-right box of the screen is the *Properties* window, which shows the properties of the screen object that is currently selected.
- The *Toolbox* is on the far-left side of the screen.

If you click on the *Toolbox* icon (Figure 5), the toolbox will open up and present a list of items. Each of these is a template for an *object* that can be placed on the *Form*. If you select one of the templates in the *Toolbox* and then drag it to the *Form*, you will place an instance of that type of object on the *Form*. In Figure 6, a *Textbox* has been placed on the form. After placing it on the form, you can use the mouse to reposition and resize the object.

Once you have multiple screen objects on the form, you can use the *Format* menu to resize, align, and position the objects to obtain a clean look for the screen.

There are several common types of screen objects that can be obtained from the *Toolbox:*

- *ListBox:* A list of values for users to select.
- *ComboBox:* A *ListBox* in which users can type a new value.
- *RadioButton:* A button that users can press, usually to select one of several possible options.
- *CheckBox:* A box that users can check if they want a particular option.

Figure 5   *Toolbox.*

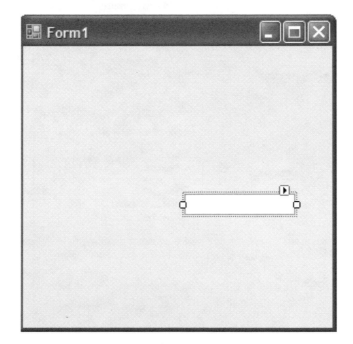

Figure 6   *TextBox on* Form.

- *Panel:* A subcanvas that other screen objects can be placed on. This is typically used to group related screen objects. A panel is often given a border to visually indicate that its screen objects are related.

When an object on the *Form* is selected, the *Properties* window will show the properties for that object (Figure 7). These will include things such as the location and size of the object. In the case of a Textbox, it will include the actual text to be displayed and the font to use for the text. When you create a screen object, the IDE will give it a default name (e.g., TextBox1). You can change any of the properties in this window, and it will change how the screen object is displayed on the form.

The following are some of the most commonly used properties:

- *Enabled:* Often used to enable/disable options on a form. If *Enabled* is false, the user cannot manipulate the object.
- *Font:* Specifies the font to be used to display text on the screen object.
- *Size:* Specifies the desired size for an object. This property can be specified in the properties window or by using the mouse to adjust the size on the design form.
- *Visible:* Can be used to dynamically change the look of a form. A screen object can be visible or invisible.

Let's look at using another item from the *Toolbox.* Place a *PictureBox* on the *Form.* A *PictureBox* can display an image. The important property of this type of object is the name of the file that contains the image to be displayed. Figure 8 provides an example.

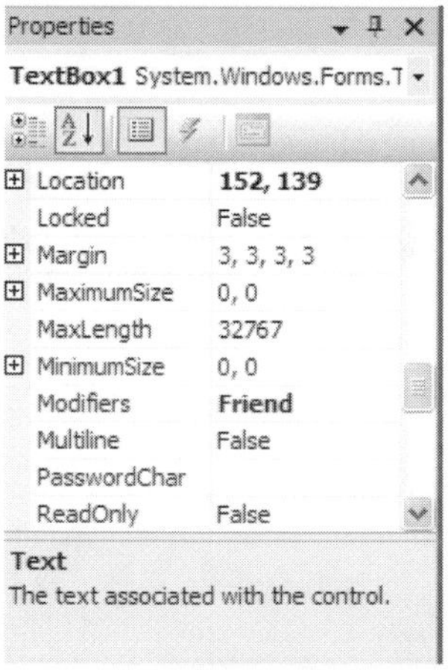

Figure 7   *Properties window for a textbox.*

Figure 8   *Using a* `PictureBox`.

Figure 9 shows a *Web Browser* screen object that shows the Web page without an address bar and other navigation features of a normal Web browser. Thus, the program is in complete control of what is shown. This is useful when information you wish to display is already available on the Web. It also allows your program to provide an interface for a data entry that is already available on the Web.

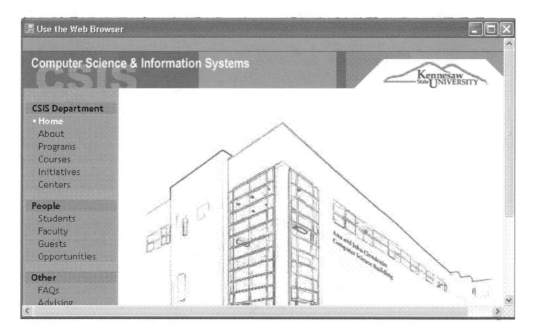

Figure 9   *Using a* `Web Browser` *screen object.*

Figure 10   *Menu and Toolbar.*

As we have seen, every screen object has a set of *Properties* and also a set of behaviors. Behaviors have two functions:

- Things that the program will do when the user interacts with it.
- Things that the program can do to interact with the screen object.

We will explore these in more detail later.

Once you have completed your *Form*, you can compile and run the program by pressing the *Run* arrow on the toolbar (see Figure 10). This will actually start Visual Basic's debugger, which will report runtime errors and allow you to examine the values of your data items.

1.2   Anatomy of a Visual Basic .NET Program

Visual Basic's *Design Screen* makes it very easy to create the visual look of an application by placing screen objects onto the window. However, in order for an application to actually do something useful, it is necessary to write code. If you press the F7 key, the *Code Window* (Figure 11) appears. This is where you place the statements that will cause the application to do something useful.

A Visual Basic Program consists of a *Class* that describes the *Form* on which you have placed screen objects. Within the class, there will be a number of subprograms (called *subroutines* in VB) to perform various functions. Some subroutines are used (or called) when you do something with one of the screen objects. These are known as *Event Subroutines*. Other subroutines will be used by the program to perform common operations. Within each subroutine, there will be a series of statements that perform the actual calculations and other operations that the program requires.

The program statements will often include reserved words (such as *If* or *Next*) that have a specific meaning in the language and cannot be used for any other purpose. In Visual Basic, reserved words begin with an initial capital letter. However, if you type a reserved word in all lowercase letters, the IDE will automatically capitalize it for you.

At the top of the *Code Window* are two dropdown menus. The one on the left has the names of screen objects in the program. When you select one of

Figure 11 *Code window.*

them, the right dropdown menu will have a list of the possible *Event Subroutines*. Most of these subroutines are rarely used. However, by selecting an appropriate event subroutine, the IDE will create skeleton code for that subroutine.

Comments in Programs

Besides the program statements, you can also include comments in a program, which always begin with an apostrophe ('). They provide information to the human reader of the program and are ignored by the Visual Basic system. Comments are as important as the language statements themselves. Consider the following two statements:

```
A = L * W          ' Multiply L and W
A = L * W          ' Compute area of rectangle
```

In the first statement, the comment provides no additional information to anybody who can read the Visual Basic language. In contrast, the comment in the second statement reveals the programmer's *intent*—extremely important additional information that often cannot be discerned from the code itself. This is one of the reasons that the program statements are sometimes called "code." In many cases, it is not obvious what is intended just by looking at the program statements. Often, you will need to go back and look at a program weeks or months after it was first written and you cannot remember (or do not know) what the intent was. Thus, the comments should provide information about *why* the program was written the way it was.

A major mistake that beginning students (and even some more experienced programmers) make is to write a program with no comments and say "I'll put the comments in later." When they do that, they do not get the benefit of the comments reminding them of their intent when they encounter a problem.

In general, comments should have two functions:

- Describe what a major section of code (e.g., a subroutine) is doing.
- Explain any nonobvious formulas or statements.

When designing a program, programmers often create English-like pseudocode to explain what is happening. It is good programming practice to convert that pseudocode into the comments for major code sections. In fact, you should do that before a single Visual Basic statement (other than maybe subroutine headers) is written.

1.3 Data Manipulation

Primitive Data Types

Primitive data types are the most basic types of data that you can work with in a program. Visual Basic supports the following primitive data types:

- *Integer:* The most common type of data that is used in programs. An integer is a whole number (no fractions) such as 29, −578, and 598765. Integers can be in the range of –2,147,483,648 to 2,147,483,647. You can also specify other types of integers such as *Byte*, *Short*, and *Long*. Like *Integer*, they cannot have a fractional part; however, they differ in the range of values that they can have.
- *Single, Double:* Values that can hold fractions and are best thought of as the computer's way of holding a number in scientific notation. Because these numbers are held in a fixed number of bits, the results of calculations can suffer from rounding errors. Examples include 3.4 and 0.56. Single values can be as small as 1.401298×10^{-45} and as large as 3.4028235×10^{38}. Double values can be as small as $4.94065645841246544 \times 10^{-324}$ and as large as $1.79769313486231570 \times 10^{308}$.
- *Decimal:* Values that provide more significant digits than *Single* or *Double* but do not have as broad a range. Unlike *Single* or *Double*, they do not have rounding errors. This data type is commonly used to represent currency values. These values can range from 0 to +/-79,228,162,514,264,337,593,543,950,335 (with no decimal places) or 0 to +/-7.9228162514264337593543950335 (with 29 decimal places).
- *Character:* Individual letters, punctuation marks, and other codes that belong to the character set of the machine. In Visual Basic, this is always UNICODE. A character constant will be specified by placing apostrophe characters around it—for example, 'a', '1', and '&'.

- *Boolean:* Typically, the result of a comparison of two values; these can be either *True* or *False.*
- *String:* A sequence of one or more characters. A *String* constant is specified by placing quotation marks around it, as in `"abc"`.

Variables, Constants, and Declarations

Each data value is stored in a location in the computer's memory. An identifier (or name) refers to each of those values. The name can be any combination of letters and digits, and underscore, but it cannot start with a digit. This is illustrated in Figure 12, which shows that the name called `Total` refers to a location in the computer memory that contains a value of 100. It is important to remember this diagram, because it will help you understand how the computer works. We will be extending this diagram in a later section when we discuss objects.

If the data value can change during the execution of the program, we refer to it as a *variable.* If it cannot change value, we call it a *constant.* To use a variable or constant in a program, you must first declare it. The *Dim* statement is used to declare variables. The declaration of a variable provides its name and its data type. Here are some examples:

```
Dim count As Integer
Dim length As Single
Dim found As Boolean
Dim name As String
```

When you declare a variable, you can optionally give it an initial value, as shown here:

```
Dim count As Integer = 0
Dim length As Single = 5.5
Dim found As Boolean = False
Dim name As String = "John Doe"
```

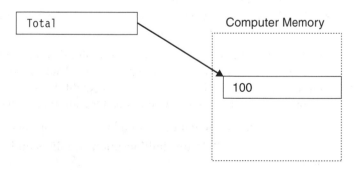

Figure 12 *Values stored in memory.*

The declaration of a constant provides its name, type, and value:

```
Const NumberTries As Integer = 5
Const Pi As Single = 3.14159265
Const FeetPerMile As Integer = 5280
```

You will often want to use the properties of a screen object as variables. To reference one of these properties, specify the name of the object, a period, and then the name of the property. Thus `Textbox1.text` refers to the text that is currently displayed in that textbox. You do not need to declare these properties yourself. That has already been done by the system when you placed the screen object onto the form.

Algebraic Expressions and Assignment

Expressions are very similar to what you learned in algebra:

- Negative values are represented by placing a minus sign ([–]) before the value.
- Addition is represented by a plus sign (+).
- Subtraction is represented by a minus sign (–)
- Multiplication is represented by an asterisk (*), which is a little different than what is done in algebra. In algebra, if you want to multiply x and y, you write xy. However, Visual Basic will interpret that as referring to the variable named xy. Thus x times y would be written as `x * y`.
- In Visual Basic, a formula must fit on one line. Thus, the exponentiation operator (^) would be used to indicate x^2, which would be written `x^2`.
- In algebra, a horizontal line indicates division, as in $\frac{x}{y}$. Because the formula must fit on one line in Visual Basic, a slash indicates division. Thus, x divided by y would be `x / y`.
- Visual Basic also has an integer division operator (\). If you use this operator, the result will have any fractional part thrown away. Thus, `5 \ 3` will have a result of 1.
- The *Mod* operator computes the remainder from integer division. Thus `5 Mod 3` will have a result of 2.

Expressions are evaluated left to right, with multiplication and division having higher precedence than addition and subtraction. That means that you will do the multiplications and divisions before the additions and subtractions. You can, of course, force the order of operations by using parentheses:

`x - y * z` will do the multiplication before the subtraction.

`a * b + c / d` will do the multiplication and division before the addition.

`a * (b + c) / d` will do the addition and then the multiplication and division.

You can change the value of a variable by using an *assignment statement*, which will have the name of a variable followed by an equal sign (=) followed by an expression.

```
z = 5        'stores the value 5 into the memory location for z.
x = y + z    'computes the sum of y and z and stores that value in x.
found = True 'changes the value in the memory location for found to be True
```

In addition to the arithmetic operators discussed above, there is also a string concatenation operator (&). This operator causes two strings to be concatenated to create one new string:

```
"abc" & "def" will create a new String "abcdef"
```

Data Type Conversion

In the course of working with data, you will often need to convert it from one data type to another. In general, there are two types of conversions:

- *Widening conversion:* A type of conversion that occurs when a data item is converted from one data type to another that has a larger range of values that can be stored. Typically, this will not cause any problems. The compiler will often handle these conversions automatically for you.
- *Narrowing conversion:* A type of conversion that stores the value into a data type that holds a smaller range of values. If the value you are converting is outside the range of values that can be held by the new data type, this will cause an error.

Data type conversions can be done automatically by the compiler when you assign a value of one data type to a variable of a different type. They can also be done automatically in the middle of an expression. For example, if you add a *Single* and an *Integer*, the compiler will automatically convert the *Integer* to *Single* before doing the addition.

Data type conversions can also be done explicitly by the programmer. Explicit conversions are typically used when you have a narrowing conversion and you know that the value is in the range of the narrower data type. Explicit conversion is performed by using one of the following conversion functions:

Function	Converts value to
CBool	*Boolean*
CByte	*Byte*
CChar	*Character*
CDbl	*Double*
CDec	*Decimal*
CInt	*Integer*
CLng	*Long*
CShort	*Short*
CSngl	*Single*
CStr	*String*

Conversions to and from *String* are typically handled automatically by Visual Basic. It is usually necessary to specify details of the conversion to *String* only when you want to control how the string will appear. For example, there are several functions available to format data:

- `FormatNumber` will produce a string with 2 digits after the decimal.
- `FormatCurrency` will produce currency such as dollars and cents.
- `FormatPercent` will format the number as a percentage.

Figure 13 shows a simple *Form* and the code to calculate Celsius temperatures from Fahrenheit temperatures. The code in this example has a subroutine header (line 5), which will be discussed in Section 6. The code in line 7 does the following:

- It obtains the Fahrenheit temperature from the text property of the Fahrenheit textbox.
- It calculates the Celsius temperature.
- It stores the result into the text property of the Celsius field.

The Fahrenheit and Celsius screen objects display strings. Visual Basic automatically performs the conversions between *String* and numeral values.

1.4 Conditional Statements

A conditional statement allows the program to conditionally select a group of statements to execute. It first evaluates a logical expression and then determines what to do based on whether that logical expression is *True* or *False*. Conditional statements come in two forms:

```
If condition Then
     statements
End if
```

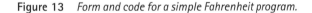

```
1  Public Class Form1
2      '
3      ' This subroutine is called by the system when the user presses the Enter button
4      '
5      Private Sub go_Enter(ByVal sender As Object, ByVal e As System.EventArgs) Handles go.Enter
6          ' Perform the calculation to convert Fahrenheit to Celsius
7          Celsius.Text = (Fahrenheit.Text - 32) * 5 / 9
8      End Sub
9  End Class
```

Figure 13   *Form and code for a simple Fahrenheit program.*

```
If condition Then
     statements
Else
     statements
End if
```

In the first form (If Then), the statements after the Then are executed if the condition is True. If the condition is False, then they are skipped. In the second form (If Then Else), if the condition is True, the statements after the Then are executed and the statements after the Else are skipped. If the condition is False, the statements after the Then are skipped and the statements after the Else are executed.

The conditions that can be used in an `If` statement are typically logical comparisons, such as `a > b`. The logical comparisons shown below are available:

=	Compares two values to see if they are equal.
<>	Compares two values to see if they are not equal.
>	Compares two values to see if the first is greater than the second.
>=	Compares two values to see if the first is greater than or equal to the second.
<	Compares two values to see if the first is less than the second.
<=	Compares two values to see if the first is less than or equal to the second.

It is possible to have multiple logical comparisons in one condition and combine them with the following:

And	Both comparisons must be true for the overall condition to be true.
Or	Either comparison can be true for the overall condition to be true.

```
If A > B And B > C Then
    statements
End If
```

If you want the opposite of one of these conditions (as in not equal), you can put the word `Not` before the condition, as in:

```
If Not (A>B And B>C) Then
```

It is also possible to have nested `If` statements. In this situation, the statements inside an `If` are also an `If`, as in:

```
If a > b Then
    If b > c Then
        Z = 10
    End If
End If
```

The nested `If` statements can occur in either the `Then` clause or the `Else` clause of an `If` statement.

Figure 14 expands the previous code example to show some examples of conditional statements. Lines 10 and 20 show simple comparisons. Line 15 shows the use of `And` to combine two logical comparisons into one `If` statement. Figure 15 expands this example to include nested `If` statements.

```
 1 ⊟ Public Class Form1
 2 ⊟     '
 3 │     ' This subroutine is called by the system when the user presses the Enter button
 4 ⊦     '
 5 ⊟     Private Sub go_Enter(ByVal sender As Object, ByVal e As System.EventArgs) Handles go.Enter
 6 │         ' Perform the calculation to convert Fahrenheit to Celsius
 7 │         celsius.Text = (fahrenheit.Text - 32) * 5 / 9
 8 │
 9 │         ' Check to see if temperature is below "Freezing"
10 │         If (fahrenheit.Text < 32) Then
11 │             comment.Text = "Water freezes."
12 │         End If
13 │
14 │         ' Check to see if temperature is above Freezing and below Boiling
15 │         If (fahrenheit.Text >= 32 And fahrenheit.Text < 212) Then
16 │             comment.Text = "Water is liquid."
17 │         End If
18 │         '
19 │         ' Is temperature above boiling?
20 │         If (fahrenheit.Text >= 212) Then
21 │             comment.Text = "Water boils."
22 │         End If
23 ⊦     End Sub
24 └ End Class
```

Figure 14   *Example of conditional statements.*

```
 1  Public Class Form1
 2        '
 3        ' This subroutine is called by the system when the user presses the Enter button
 4        '
 5        Private Sub go_Enter(ByVal sender As Object, ByVal e As System.EventArgs) Handles go.Enter
 6            ' Perform the calculation to convert Fahrenheit to Celsius
 7            celsius.Text = (fahrenheit.Text - 32) * 5 / 9
 8
 9            ' Check to see if temperature is below "Freezing"
10            If (fahrenheit.Text < 32) Then
11                comment.Text = "Water freezes."
12            End If
13
14            ' Check to see if temperature is above Freezing and below Boiling
15            If (fahrenheit.Text >= 32 And fahrenheit.Text < 212) Then
16                comment.Text = "Water is liquid."
17
18                ' Check for finer temerature ranges to add an additional comment
19                '
20                If (fahrenheit.Text < 45) Then
21                    comment.Text = comment.Text + " You need a Jacket."
22                End If
23                If (fahrenheit.Text >= 45 And fahrenheit.Text < 90) Then
24                    comment.Text = comment.Text + " It's Comfortable weather"
25                End If
26                If (fahrenheit.Text >= 90 And fahrenheit.Text < 120) Then
27                    comment.Text = comment.Text + "You're going to sweat"
28                End If
29                If (fahrenheit.Text >= 120) Then
30                    comment.Text = comment.Text + " Even rattlesnakes can't move"
31                End If
32            End If
33            '
34            ' Is temperature above boiling?
35            If (fahrenheit.Text >= 212) Then
36                comment.Text = "Water boils."
37            End If
38        End Sub
39  End Class
```

Figure 15   *Nested conditional statements.*

1.5   Looping Statements

A looping statement allows you to repeat the same group of statements multiple times. There are several forms of looping statements:

```
Do While condition
     statements
Loop

Do
     statements
Loop While condition

For variable=initial <Step increment> to endValue
     Statements
Next
```

In the first form (*Do While*), the condition is evaluated. If it is *True*, the statements are executed and then the *Do While* statement is repeated. If the condition is *False*, the loop is complete and the program will then execute whatever statements are after the *Loop* statement.

In the second form (*Do Loop*), the statements are executed and then the condition is evaluated. If the condition is *True*, the program will loop back and repeat the statements again. If the condition is *False*, the program is done with the loop and will execute whatever follows the *Loop While* statement.

The third form (*For*) has a counter variable that is incremented each time through the loop. You can specify the amount that the variable is incremented in the optional *Step* clause. If the *Step* clause is missing, you default to an increment of 1. The program will repeatedly execute the statements and then increment the counter variable until the end condition is *True*.

The examples shown in Figures 16 through 18 illustrate the calculation of the factorial function using each of the three types of looping statements.

```
1 Public Class Form1
2
3     Private Sub Calculate_Enter(ByVal sender As Object, ByVal e As System.EventArgs) Handles Calculate.Enter
4         ' This program shows a While loop calculating N factorial
5
6         ' We use a counter, starting at 1 and going up to N
7         Dim Counter As Integer = 1
8
9         ' Integer version of N
10        Dim N As Integer = CInt(NDisplay.Text)
11
12        ' Factorial caluclation starts at 1 and multiplies up
13        Dim Factorial As Integer = 1
14
15        Do While (Counter <= N)
16            ' Calculate the value of Counter factorial
17            Factorial = Counter * Factorial
18            ' Increment the counter
19            Counter = Counter + 1
20        Loop
21
22        ' Store the final result onto the Form
23        FactorialDisplay.Text = CStr(Factorial)
24    End Sub
25 End Class
```

Figure 16 *Factorial using* `While` *statement.*

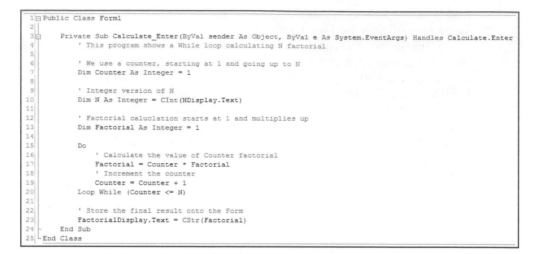

```
 1 Public Class Form1
 2
 3     Private Sub Calculate_Enter(ByVal sender As Object, ByVal e As System.EventArgs) Handles Calculate.Enter
 4         ' This program shows a While loop calculating N factorial
 5
 6         ' We use a counter, starting at 1 and going up to N
 7         Dim Counter As Integer = 1
 8
 9         ' Integer version of N
10         Dim N As Integer = CInt(NDisplay.Text)
11
12         ' Factorial caluclation starts at 1 and multiplies up
13         Dim Factorial As Integer = 1
14
15         Do
16             ' Calculate the value of Counter factorial
17             Factorial = Counter * Factorial
18             ' Increment the counter
19             Counter = Counter + 1
20         Loop While (Counter <= N)
21
22         ' Store the final result onto the Form
23         FactorialDisplay.Text = CStr(Factorial)
24     End Sub
25 End Class
```

Figure 17   *Factorial using* `Do while`.

```
 1 Public Class Form1
 2
 3     Private Sub Calculate_Enter(ByVal sender As Object, ByVal e As System.EventArgs) Handles Calculate.Enter
 4         ' This program shows a While loop calculating N factorial
 5
 6         ' Integer version of N
 7         Dim N As Integer = CInt(NDisplay.Text)
 8
 9         ' Factorial calculation starts at 1 and multiplies up
10         Dim Factorial As Integer = 1
11
12         For counter As Integer = 1 To N
13             ' Calculate the value of Counter factorial
14             Factorial = counter * Factorial
15         Next
16
17         ' Store the final result onto the Form
18         FactorialDisplay.Text = CStr(Factorial)
19     End Sub
20 End Class
```

Figure 18   *Factorial using* `For` *loop.*

Generally, you can determine which type of looping structure to use by these steps:

1. Do you know (or can calculate) how many times to execute the loop? If yes, use a *For*.
2. Do you know whether you should execute the loop at least once? If yes, use a *Do While*.
3. Otherwise, use a *Loop While*.

Just as you can have nested *If* statements, you can also have nested loops.

1.6 Subroutines and Functions

Subroutines and *Functions* are named sections of code that can be called (used) at other places in the program. They perform two useful functions:

- Repeat the same operation in many different places.
- Break up a large and complex program into smaller, more understandable pieces.

The difference between a *Subroutine* and a *Function* is that a *Function* will return a computed value to the place in the program from which it was called. To use a *Subroutine* or *Function*, you can "call" the *Subroutine/Function* with the actual values it must use for its parameters at that point in the program. There are many library *Subroutines* and *Functions* that come with Visual Basic, including the following two examples:

MsgBox	Displays a dialog box with a message for the user.
Math.Sqrt	Computes the square root of a value.

When we call a *Subroutine* or *Function*, we need to pass it any values that are required for it to perform its desired operation. For example, we need to pass to MsgBox the *String* that we want to have displayed in the box. Similarly, we need to pass to Sqrt the value whose square root we would like to have calculated. These parameters are specified in the *Subroutine/Function* header by the developer who wrote the *Subroutine* or *Function.*

You specify a *Subroutine* with the following:

```
Sub name (parameters)
     statements
End Sub
```

You specify a *Function* with

```
Function name (parameters) As type
     statements
     Return value
End Function
```

The function declaration specifies the data type of the value that it will return to the calling program. The last executable statement in the function is a *Return* statement that provides the actual value to be returned to the calling program.

The parameters specify values that the calling program needs to provide to the *Subroutine* or *Function* in order for the *Subroutine* to perform its desired calculations. The parameter declaration is a list of variable declarations that provide the names and data types of the parameter variables as they are to be used in the *Subroutine*. When the main program wishes to use the *Subroutine*, it specifies the name of the *Subroutine* and a list of values to be passed to the *Subroutine*. The compiler effectively causes these values to be assigned to the parameter variables at the beginning of the *Subroutine*.

When you write a *Subroutine* specification header, the Visual Basic IDE will add the reserved word *ByVal* at the beginning of each parameter declaration. This means that the value of that parameter will not be passed back to the calling program (even if it has been changed in the *Subroutine*). In advanced programming, it is possible to change this.

Events

The typical Visual Basic program is built around the idea of handling *Events*—actions that happen outside the direct control of the program. Usually, this will be the user performing some action on the screen *Form* (e.g., typing some information or clicking on a button). However, there are other types of events, such as a timer period elapsing or the initial loading of a program.

Events are handled in *Event Subroutines*, which are created by using the dropdown menu at the top of the *Code Window* in the Visual Basic development environment. Commonly, you will create *Event Subroutines* for any buttons that are on the form. These subroutines will be called when a button is pressed, and they should have the statements required to achieve whatever is defined for that button. Other *Event Subroutines* will be created for other components that require some programming action when they occur. Figure 19 shows the *Event Subroutine* for the *Enter Event* for the button in our Fahrenheit program. The subroutine header was created by selecting *Go Events* in the left dropdown menu and *Enter* in the right dropdown menu.

Another commonly used *Event Subroutine* is the *Form Load Event* handler. This subroutine is typically used to perform any initialization for the form that cannot be achieved simply by setting the properties of the screen objects on the form.

```
1 Public Class Form1
2     '
3     ' This subroutine is called by the system when the user presses the Enter button
4     '
5     Private Sub go_Enter(ByVal sender As Object, ByVal e As System.EventArgs) Handles go.Enter
6         ' Perform the calculation to convert Fahrenheit to Celsius
7         Celsius.Text = (Fahrenheit.Text - 32) * 5 / 9
8     End Sub
9 End Class
```

Figure 19 *Event Subroutine* for a button.

1.7 Collections of Data

Using Classes

A *Class* describes an *object*, which is a collection of related information in memory (see Figure 20). Visual Basic has many built-in classes for you to use. In a later section, you will learn how to create your own classes. An object is created from a class template, which describes the information that the object should contain. In this example, the object is created from a `Person` class.

Additionally, the object will have a set of *Subroutines* (and/or *Functions*) that can be used to manipulate the data in the object. In the example above, there may be a "pay" subroutine that will print a paycheck for the employee. To create an object from the class template, use the *New* operator. Thus, for the example above, you may have

```
employee = New Person("James, 23, 10000)
```

You can access the data and subroutines of the object by using the name of the object, a dot, and the name of the data or subroutine:

`employee.Age` would obtain the employee's age.

`employee.pay()` would call the pay subroutine to print that employee's paycheck.

When using a class from a library that is not part of the Visual Basic standard libraries, you must inform the compiler where to find the library. You use the imports statement for this. The imports statement(s) must be the very first thing in the code file. For example, the following statement is required to use some of the graphics features described later:

```
Imports System.drawing.drawing2D
```

Figure 20 An *Object* in memory.

Arrays and ArrayLists

Often, there may be a group of similar values (e.g., the scores on a test). Rather than having a unique variable name for each of these values, you can store all of the values into one array and then access the individual elements of the array. For example, if you have ten scores, you can place those ten values into an array called "scores" (see Figure 21). You can then access individual elements of that array using an index number. Note that the elements of the array have index values that begin with 0 (not 1).

When declaring an array variable, specify the upper bound (i.e., the index of the last element) as well as the data type of the array elements, as in this example:

```
Dim scores(9) As Integer
Dim speeds(100) As Single
```

Note that all of the elements of the array are of the same data type. If you have a situation in which you have related data values that are of different types, you need to use a class (described later).

To use an array element, specify the name of the array and the index of the element you want to use. The index value can be a constant, a variable, or any integer expression, as in this example:

```
Scores(5) = 67

For I As Integer = 0 to 99
    Total = Total + scores(I)
Next
```

For Each is another form of the *For* statement that is extremely useful when working with arrays. The example from above can be rewritten as follows:

```
For Each score in scores
    Total = Total + score
Next
```

The *For Each* statement avoids the necessity of keeping track of the array index and its limit. Instead, you specify a variable name and an array name. Each time through the loop, the variable will receive the value of the next element of

Scores	29	54	89	73	93	67	81	91	88	71
Index	0	1	2	3	4	5	6	7	8	9

Figure 21   *An example array.*

```
 1 Public Class Form1
 2     ' ArrayList to hold data values
 3     ' ArrayLis tis used becuase it can expand and contract
 4     Dim dataValues As New ArrayList
 5
 6     ' Event Subroutine called when user presses Add button
 7     Private Sub AddButton_Click(ByVal sender As Object, ByVal e As System.EventArgs) Handles AddButton.Click
 8         ' Add data value from from to our ArrayList
 9         dataValues.Add(Data.Text)
10     End Sub
11
12     ' Event subroutine called when user presses Remove button
13     Private Sub RemoveButton_Click(ByVal sender As Object, ByVal e As System.EventArgs) Handles RemoveButton.Click
14         ' Remove data value specified by the form |
15         dataValues.Remove(Data.Text)
16     End Sub
17 End Class
```

Figure 22 ArrayList *example.*

the array. The loop will process all of the elements of the array. Note that *For Each* is useful only when you do not need to use the array index. Generally, that means you can use it when accessing the array elements, but not when you are changing them.

Arrays are a very efficient approach to handling situations where the number of data elements is fixed. If you need to add new elements to the array as time goes on or remove elements from the array, a lot of additional code is required to handle the situation.

Visual Basic has a built-in class called *ArrayList*, which will handle these situations for you. Figure 22 shows an example. Line 4 is a declaration of a variable (`dataValues`), which will refer to an *ArrayList* that is created by using `New`. Line 9 adds a value to the *ArrayList* (at the end of the list). You can also insert a value into the middle. Line 15 removes a value.

ArrayList is a commonly used example of what is known as a collections class (i.e., it keeps track of a collection of data). Just as you could use *For* loops (including *For Each*) with arrays, you can use them with collections also.

Defining Classes

Arrays and *ArrayLists* are convenient ways of organizing related data items that have the same data type. Often, you must deal with related data items that have different data types. For example, it may be necessary to maintain information about a student:

- Name—a String
- Age—an Integer
- Address—a String
- Test scores—Integers

In addition, there may be many students and you may want to keep the information for each student together. You can organize the related information for a student in an object, which is described in the program by a class.

A program consists of one or more classes. The screen form that is created for you by the Visual Basic IDE when you begin a project is actually a class. Each of the items in the toolbox is also a class. You can think of a class as a template or pattern for one or more objects that will be created when you run the program. While you can create many programs using just these predefined classes, as we just saw, it is often useful to create your own classes.

A class looks like this:

```
Class className
    variable declarations
    subroutines and functions
End Class
```

The variables declared immediately after the class header are called *instance variables.* That term refers to the fact that each object created from the class has its own set of variables (and associated values) from those declared here. Consider the following example, which is a class that is used to represent the values for a student:

```
Class Student
    dim name As String
    dim age As Integer
    dim address As String
    dim testScores() As Integer
End Class
```

If you have two different students, then each object will have variables called name, age, address, and testScores, but they will have different values.

The constructor is a special subroutine whose name is New. The constructor is called with slightly different syntax, as in this example:

```
Dim jane As Student
jane = New Student( "James", 19, "123 Elm St")
```

The constructor subroutine for this example would look like this:

```
Class Student
    Dim name As String
    Dim age As Integer
    dim address As String
    dim testScores() As Integer

    Public sub New(studentName As String,
                   studentAge As Integer,
                   studentAddress As String)
        name = studentName
        age = studentAge
        address = studentAddress
    End Sub
End Class
```

The constructor will do two things:

- Allocate the memory space for the new object. This is done automatically by Visual Basic.
- Initialize the values for the object's instance variables. Often, these values are passed to the constructor in parameters for the "New" subroutine, as in the above example.

A class will have data values and subroutines. Subroutines are specified in the same way as already shown.

Encapsulation

Encapsulation is the concept that a user of a class should have access only to the information and subroutines it needs in order to do its job. In general, this means you want to tightly control access to the instance variables of the objects created from the class.

Normally, names for variables/constants, subroutines/function, and classes are known within the entity that contains the declaration. This means that you can assume the following:

- Variables declared inside a subroutine/function are known only inside that subroutine/function.
- Variables and subroutines/functions declared in a class are known only within the class.

The visibility of items declared in a class can be changed by using a visibility modifier in the declaration:

- *Public* says the item is visible to the whole world.
- *Private* says the item is visible only within the class.

If you declare an instance variable with a *Dim* statement, Visual Basic treats it as *Private*. However, it is desirable to use the word *Private* to emphasize that it is not *Public*.

To achieve encapsulation, it is highly recommended that you not have public instance variables. However, you typically want to provide some access to the data in the object. This can be done with *Properties*, which are specified as shown here:

```
Public Property name As data type
    Get
        statements
    End Get
    Set (parameters)
        statements
    End Set
End Property
```

This specifies the data type of the property and two subroutines: one to get the value of the *Property* and another to set the value of the *Property*. To get the value of a *Property*, you specify `objectName.propertyname`. Similarly, you can set the value of the property by putting `objectName.propertyname` on the left side of an assignment statement.

Properties provide a number of nice features to enhance encapsulation:

- The *Set* subroutine can validate that a legal value is being stored.
- The *Set* subroutine can perform calculations and actually change multiple data values.
- The *Property* can be specified as *ReadOnly* so that other classes can access the *Property* but not change it.
- *Properties* can be defined for values that are calculated but not stored. For example, an object might store values in metric units, but have *Properties* defined that get and set values in inches.

Figure 23 shows an example of a *Property* being used to validate that a legal value is being stored into an instance variable. Line 413 verifies that a positive value has been provided, and then the value is stored in line 414 into the private instance variable declared in line 404. With this set of declarations, this property can then be used in the following manner:

```
Dim aFigure As New Figure()

    ' Set the Layer to 1
    aFigure.Layer = 1

    ' Retrieve the layer
    x = aFigure.Layer
```

```
402 Public Class Figure
403     ' Canvas layer this Figure is on
404     Private iLayer As Integer
405
406     ' Layer property
407     ' Validates that Layer is positive
408     Public Property Layer() As Integer
409         Get
410             Layer = iLayer
411         End Get
412         Set(ByVal value As Integer)
413             If (value >= 0) Then
414                 iLayer = value
415             End If
416         End Set
417     End Property
```

Figure 23 *Use of* Property.

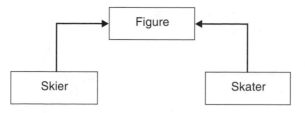

Figure 24 *Inheritance.*

Notice that while we define a property in terms of *Get* and *Set* subroutines, they are treated like variables by the user of the *Property*.

Inheritance and Polymorphism

Inheritance is the concept that you can build one class on top of another. In this situation, you can say that one class inherits the features of the other. In particular, a child class inherits the features of a parent class. Syntactically, this done with the *Inherits* clause:

```
Public Class Skater
     Inherits Figure
End Class

Public Class Skier
     Inherits Figure
End Class
```

This says that the classes called `Skater` and `Skier` will have all of the data and subroutines of the class called `Figure`, as well as any that are defined within each of them. We can usually think of the child as a more specific example of the general parent class. This is illustrated in Figure 24.

Polymorphism is the concept that if you are dealing with the attributes (data and subroutines) of a class, you really do not care if the object is actually an instance of that class or one of its children. In the example above, if you are dealing with the attributes of `Figure`, it doesn't matter whether the object is an instance of `Skater`, `Skier`, or `Figure`. For example, suppose `Figure` has an attribute (property) of weight. Then `Skier` and `Skater` will also have that property. Thus, if you are interested in that property, you do not care whether the object is actually a `Skier` or a `Skater`.

1.8 Graphics

Colors are typically represented as a combination of *Red*, *Green*, and *Blue*. The values for each color will range from 0 to 255, with 0 meaning that there is none of that primary color and 255 that there is the maximum amount. Thus 0,0,0 means black and 255,255,255 means white. Visual Basic simplifies the specification of common values by having predefined definitions for the common colors. Thus `Color.Red` specifies *Red*.

The screen is painted with a series of dots called *pixels*. Each pixel has a position (or *screen coordinate*). This is similar to the rectangular coordinates that you learned in geometry, with one important difference. On the screen, the (0, 0) coordinate is the upper-left corner. Increasing values on the *y* axis move down (not *up* as in geometry class). In Figure 25, the arrows point to a pixel that is 150 across and 100 down from the upper-left corner of the screen.

Each screen object (including the *Form*) has a *Paint Event* associated with it. This *Event* is called whenever the system wishes to draw that object. By defining your own *Paint Event Subroutine*, you can draw whatever you wish for that screen object. The *Paint Event Subroutine* is passed a *Graphics* object as a parameter. This object provides the canvas upon which you will do your drawing. It also provides the methods used to do the drawing. Figure 26 shows a paint event subroutine that draws a rectangle on the screen.

To draw a line, you can use a *Pen*, which has a *Color* and a *Width* of the line it draws. While it is possible to create your own *Pen*, Visual Basic has a large set of predefined *Pens* such as `Pens.Red`. In addition to drawing lines, you can fill screen images such as rectangles and ellipses with a color. This is done with *Brushes*, which can either be a solid color or much more complex colors that change their shade as they move across the screen. Visual Basic has a set of predefined brushes, as in `Brushes.Red`.

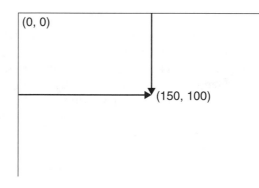

Figure 25 *Screen coordinates.*

```
1 Public Class Form1
2
3     Private Sub Form1_Paint(ByVal sender As Object, ByVal e As System.Windows.Forms.PaintEventArgs)
4         Dim g As Graphics = e.Graphics
5         g.DrawRectangle(Pens.Red, 50, 100, 40, 80)
6     End Sub
7 End Class
```

Figure 26 *Example of a* `Paint Event` *handler.*

The common methods that the *Graphics* object provides are shown in the table below.

`drawLine` (pen, x1, y1, x2, y2)	Draws a line from point (x1,x2) to point (x2,y2).
`drawRectangle` (pen, x, y, width, height)	Draws a rectangle with its upper-left corner at point (x,y) and specified width and height.
`drawEllipse` (pen, x, y, width, height)	Draws an ellipse that is bounded by an imaginary rectangle whose upper-left corner is at point (x,y) and has specified width and height.
`drawPolygon` (pen, point array)	Draws a polygon whose points are specified in the point array. Each element of that array is a Point object that specifies an x and y coordinate.
`drawString` (text, font, x, y)	Draws the text on the screen using the specified font.
`fillRectangle` (brush, x, y, width, height)	Same as `drawRectangle` except that the brush is used to fill the rectangle.
`fillEllipse` (brush, x, y, width, height)	Same as `drawEllipse` except that the brush is used to fill the ellipse.
`fillPolygon` (brush, point array)	Same as `drawPolygon` except that the brush is used to fill the polygon.

Summary

Visual Basic .Net 2005 is the latest version of Microsoft's Visual Basic programming language/development environment. It combines an easy-to-use interactive development environment with an object-oriented programming language. As provided by Microsoft, it is a good introductory programming language. When combined with the vast libraries of additional classes that are available, it becomes an extremely powerful programming tool that can be used to interact with databases and spreadsheets as well as to communicate over the Internet.

Exercises

1. Create and run a program that has a *Textbox* with your name in 20pt Helvetica Italic font. Do the same thing with a *Label* from the *Toolbox*. What is the difference between these two objects?

2. Pick any image and use a *PictureBox* to display it. You will need to set the image property to specify the file that contains the image you wish to display. You may need to adjust the size of the *PictureBox* and/or the *Form* for your entire picture to display.

3. Use the *MonthCalendar* to display a calendar. Run the program. What can you do with the calendar? What happens if you change the `TodayDate` property and then run the program?

4. Use the *WebBrowser* control to display a Web page. You will need to set the URL property to specify the address of the Web page.

5. Write a program that accepts three numbers from the user and displays their average.

6. Write a program that accepts an `age` from the user and then displays one of `Child`, `Teenager`, `Adult`, `Senior Citizen`, depending on the value of `age`.

7. Enhance the program from above so that if the person is a `Teenager`, it will print whether he is old enough to drive.

8. Change the program from above so that the code to determine whether the person is a `Child`, `Teenager`, etc., is in a function (that is, the function returns the string that should be displayed).

9. Write a *Do While* loop that adds the integers –10 to –2.

10. Write a *For* loop that add the integers –10 to –2.

11. Write a program that displays the average of the values in an array.

12. Write a program that has users enter a value and adds that value to an *ArrayList* when they click a button. Thus the *ArrayList* continually grows. Have another button that causes the specified value to be removed from the *ArrayList*.

13. Enhance the *ArrayList* program from above to display the contents of the *ArrayList* in a *Listbox*.

14. Change the *ListBox* to a *ComboBox* and use the *ComboBox* for the user to add values to the list.

15. Write an `Employee` class that has *Properties* for the various values.

16. Write `SalariedEmployee` and `HourlyEmployee` classes that are subclasses of the `Employee` class.

17. Use the graphics features to draw a house.

18. Use the graphics features to draw a stick figure. Use the `Timer` object from the `Toolbox` to change the position on the screen of the stick figure.

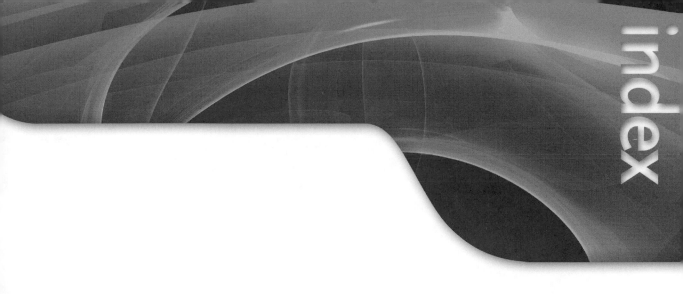